HAL•LEONARD
INSTRUMENTAL PLAY-ALONG

AUDIO
ACCESS
INCLUDED

PLAYBACK+
eed • Pitch • Balance • Loop

FLUTE

by SCHULZ

T0056336

To access audio visit:
www.halleonard.com/mylibrary

Enter Code
2832-0227-9066-6855

Visit Peanuts® on the internet at
www.snoopy.com

ISBN 978-1-4234-8686-2

HAL•LEONARD®
7777 W. BLUEMOUND RD. P.O. BOX 13819 MILWAUKEE, WI 53213

Visit Hal Leonard Online at
www.halleonard.com

TITLE	PAGE

BLUE CHARLIE BROWN

Flute

By VINCE GUARALDI

CHARLIE BROWN THEME

Flute

By VINCE GUARALDI

CHARLIE'S BLUES

FLUTE

By VINCE GUARALDI

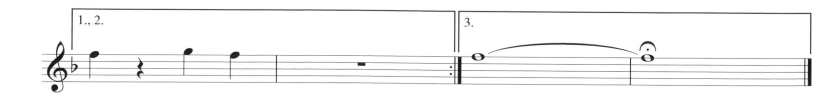

CHRISTMAS TIME IS HERE

Flute

Words by LEE MENDELSON
Music by VINCE GUARALDI

CHRISTMAS IS COMING

FLUTE

By VINCE GUARALDI

THE GREAT PUMPKIN WALTZ

Flute

By VINCE GUARALDI

JOE COOL

Flute

By VINCE GUARALDI

LINUS AND LUCY

Flute

By VINCE GUARALDI

JUST LIKE ME

Flute

Lyrics by LEE MENDELSON
Music by DAVID BENOIT

MY LITTLE DRUM

Flute

By VINCE GUARALDI

O TANNENBAUM

Flute

Traditional
Arranged by VINCE GUARALDI

OH, GOOD GRIEF

Flute

By VINCE GUARALDI

SKATING

By VINCE GUARALDI

FLUTE

RED BARON

Flute

By VINCE GUARALDI

WHAT CHILD IS THIS

Flute

Traditional
Arranged by VINCE GUARALDI